spot

ARCTIC ANIMAL

D1276749

SNOWY OWLS

by Anastasia Suen

AMICUS | AMICUS INK

feathers

beak

Look for these words and pictures as you read.

eyes

talons

Do you see that bird?
It's a snowy owl.
It lives in the Arctic.

See the feathers?
Some are brown.
Some are white.

feathers

Males have more white feathers.
Females have more brown.

See the beak?

It is covered in feathers.

The beak stays warm.

beak

eyes

See the eyes?
They look for food.
They can look behind the owl.

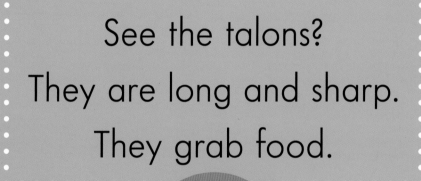

See the talons?
They are long and sharp.
They grab food.

talons

A snowy owl sits in a nest.
It cuddles a baby chick.

feathers

beak

Did you find?

eyes

talons

spot

Spot is published by Amicus and Amicus Ink
P.O. Box 1329, Mankato, MN 56002
www.amicuspublishing.us

Cataloging-in-Publication Data is available from the
Library of Congress
978-1-68151-800-8 (library bound)
978-1-68152-528-0 (paperback)
978-1-68151-840-4 (eBook)

Printed in China

HC 10 9 8 7 6 5 4 3 2 1
PB   10 9 8 7 6 5 4 3 2 1

Alissa Thielges, editor
Deb Miner, series designer
Ciara Beitlich, book designer
Holly Young and Shane Freed,
   photo researchers

Photos by iStock/pchoui cover, 16;
iStock/ca2hill 1; Getty/Danita Delimont
3; WikiMedia Commons/Frank Vassen
4–5; Alamy/Martin Smart 6–7; iStock/
Stephen_Lavery 8–9; Getty/Corey
Hardcastle 10–11; Alamy/Miguel Lasa/
Steve Bloom Images 12–13; Newscom/J.
Peltomaeki 14–15

SNOWY OWLS